Le guide del gabbiano

W9-DJD-278

Italian
for travellers

CONVERSATION
HANDBOOK

 4000 WORDS

 2000 PHRASES

GIUNTI

project
Paolo Piazzesi

editing
Christiane Splinter

translation
Michael Barbour
Colleen Campbell
Stephanie Johnson

phonetics
Leonardo Lavacchi

cover
Rocío Isabel Gonzàlez

graphic design
Fabio Campetti BCP Associati Designers, Firenze

illustrations
Stefano Grisieti, Studio Bertram, Firenze

impagination
Thèsis S.r.l., Firenze

© 1999, Giunti Gruppo Editoriale, Firenze
ISBN 88-09-217640